CamJansen

The School Play Mystery

David A. Adler

Illustrated by Susanna Natti

This edition is published by special arrangement with Puffin Books, A Division of Penguin Young Readers Group, A Member of Penguin Group (USA) Inc.

Grateful acknowledgment is made to Puffin Books, A Division of Penguin Young Readers Group, A Member of Penguin Group (USA) Inc. for permission to reprint *Cam Jansen: The School Play Mystery* by David A. Adler, illustrated by Susanna Natti. Text copyright © 2001 by David A. Adler; illustrations copyright © 2001 by Susanna Natti.

Printed in China

ISBN 10   0-15-356582-9
ISBN 13   978-0-15-356582-3

1 2 3 4 5 6 7 8 9 10 985 16 15 14 13 12 10 09 08 07

How could someone steal money from a sealed box?

Susie looked to the right again. Then she said, "You walked all this way to bring me six cents?" She patted Eric's shoulder and said, "Now I know why people call you Honest Abe."

Eric and Susie walked to the center of the stage and bowed. The children who had been in Offutt's Store came out and bowed, too. People in the audience clapped.

As the curtain closed, Sara said to Cam and Danny, "This is a play about Honest Abe Lincoln, but there's someone here who's not honest at all."

"He's not honest, but he's clever," Danny said. "Somehow, he stole the money without opening the box. And he stole the money without Sara or me seeing him do it."

"Ms. Benson said she was counting on me," Cam said, "and now the money is gone. I've got to tell her what happened."

CamJansen
The School Play
Mystery

To
Rachel, Shelby,
and Mathew

CHAPTER ONE

"I . . . I . . . I . . ." Eric Shelton said. "Oh, I can't do this!"

Eric looked at the papers he was holding. "It's too scary." He shook his head. "I can't do this," he said. "I just can't."

Eric wore a long black jacket, white shirt, black bow tie, and black boots. He stood on the stage of his school's auditorium. He was the star of the school play, *Stories of President Lincoln.*

"Of course you can," his friend Cam Jansen told him. "You're smart and honest. You'll make a great President Lincoln."

Eric smiled.

"I love the second half of the play," Cam told him. "I love it when you put on that top hat and beard. You look just like President Lincoln."

"But I won't remember my lines."

"Sure you will," Cam told him. "You have a great memory."

"No," Eric said. "I have a good memory. *You* have a great memory."

Now Cam smiled.

"Here," Eric said. He gave Cam his papers. "Test me. See if I know my lines."

"I don't need the script." Cam pointed to her head. "I have a picture of it right here," she said.

Cam closed her eyes and said, "*Click.*"

"It's six cents," Eric said. "I made a mistake this morning when you were in the store."

"You walked all this way to bring me six cents?" Cam asked with her eyes still closed.

Cam reached out and hit Eric's nose. "Oops! I'm sorry," Cam said.

Eric moved her hand to his shoulder.

Cam patted Eric's shoulder and said, "Now I know why people call you Honest Abe."

Eric applauded. "That was great," he said. "You know Susie's part."

Cam opened her eyes, "I know everyone's part," she said. "I have a picture in my head of every page of the script."

Eric was right. Cam does have a great memory. "I have a mental camera," she says, "and pictures in my head of just about everything I've seen."

Cam says, *"Click,"* when she wants to use her mental camera. She says *Click* is the sound her mental camera makes.

Cam's real name is Jennifer. But when people found out about her amazing memory, they began calling her "The Camera." Soon "The Camera" became just "Cam."

"Where's Susie?" Ms. Benson called out. "Where's Jane? Where's Hillel? Hurry! Hurry!"

Children ran to their places.

"Cam, is everything in order back here?"

"Yes," Cam answered.

"Good. I'm counting on you."

Ms. Benson fixed Eric's bow tie and Susie's collar. Then she told Cam, "Let's go out front."

Cam followed Ms. Benson into the hall. Two children sat there behind a table. On the table were schoolbooks, a comic book, a few animal crackers, a pile of tickets, and a shoe box.

"Sara and Danny, this is no good," Ms.

Benson said. "I want just the box and the tickets on the table."

Sara and Danny took everything else off the table.

There was a slit in the top of the shoe box. The sides were neatly taped to keep the box closed.

"The money goes in here," Ms. Benson said. She pointed to the top of the shoe box.

"And don't take off the tape. Just put the money in the box. Tickets are one dollar each, so you shouldn't have to make change."

"I think we're ready," Cam said.

Ms. Benson looked at her watch.

"OK," she told Cam. "Let's open the doors."

CHAPTER TWO

Cam turned the latch on the doors to the school yard. Ms. Benson pushed the doors open.

"Welcome. Welcome," Ms. Benson said to the people who walked in. "Just line up by the table. Sara and Danny will be happy to sell you tickets. Remember, all the money we raise goes to charity. It's for Ride and Read, to bring homebound elderly people to the library."

An old woman was the first in line. "My granddaughter is in the play," she told Sara. "She's Mary Todd Lincoln."

The next woman in line said, "My nephew is taking care of the lights. That's important, too."

Cam walked past the long line of people waiting to buy tickets. She went outside, into the school yard. Some young children were on the swings. Lots of teenagers were playing basketball.

Cam looked across the school yard. Then

she saw her parents and Eric's family. Cam waved. "Hurry," she called to them. "The play is about to start."

"This is so exciting," Mr. and Mrs. Jansen said as they entered the school.

Eric's twin sisters, Donna and Diane, were next. Then Mr. and Mrs. Shelton walked in. Mr. Shelton carried Eric's baby brother, Howie.

"Sh," Mr. Shelton whispered to Cam. "Howie is asleep."

Cam watched as her mother paid for two tickets. Danny pushed the money through the narrow slit in the top of the shoe box.

Next, the Sheltons paid for their tickets.

"Please stay here," Ms. Benson told Cam. "I'm going backstage to see if everyone is ready."

A few boys came in from the school yard. One of them carried a basketball.

"Hey, what's going on here?" one of the boys asked.

Cam told them they were raising money

for charity. She told them about the play. But they weren't interested in a play about President Lincoln.

"I learned enough about him in school," one of the boys said as they left.

There were only a few people still in line. The last was a tall woman. She had on an orange dress. Cam wanted to remember her. She looked at the woman, blinked her eyes, and said, *"Click."*

Then Cam told Sara and Danny, "I'll let Ms. Benson know you're just about done. I'll be right back."

Cam walked into the auditorium. The seats were almost all filled. It was noisy. People were talking while they waited for the play to begin.

Cam went backstage. Her classmates were checking their costumes. Some were looking at their scripts, making sure they remembered their lines.

"You all look just fine," Ms. Benson said. "We're going to put on a great play."

Susie giggled.

"What is it?" Ms. Benson asked.

"I'm sorry," Susie answered. "I laugh when I'm nervous."

"Don't be nervous," Ms. Benson said. "If you forget your lines, look to the right. I'll be just behind the curtain. I'll help you. And, please, don't laugh."

Ms. Benson asked Cam, "Is everyone seated?"

Cam looked through the curtains at the people waiting for the play to begin. She found the tall woman with the orange dress. The woman was in the aisle. She was drinking from a soda can and looking for a seat.

Cam told Ms. Benson, "We are almost ready."

Cam watched the woman with the orange dress sit in the last row.

"Now we can start," Cam said. "The last one in line for tickets just took her seat."

Ms. Benson gave Cam a pair of scissors and a leather purse. She told Cam to open the shoe box, count the money, and put it in

the purse. Then Ms. Benson called out, "Dim the lights. The show is about to begin."

Cam walked quickly down the center aisle. The lights dimmed. People in the audience stopped talking. They looked toward the stage and waited.

Cam opened the doors and went into the hall.

"Can we go in now?" Sara asked. "We want to see the play, too."

Cam said, "Ms. Benson wants us to open the box. She wants us to count the money and put it in this purse. Then we can all go in to see the play."

Cam cut the tape that was wrapped around the top and sides of the box. She took off the lid.

There were just a few dollars in the box.

"Hey," Cam said. "You sold lots of tickets. What happened to all the money?"

CHAPTER THREE

Sara counted the money. There were just three dollar bills and four quarters in the box.

"I put lots of money in there," Sara said. "Lots more than this."

Danny said, "I did, too."

"The auditorium is just about full," Cam said. "You must have sold about 150 tickets. At one dollar each, that's 150 dollars." Cam held up the money she had taken from the box. "All we have here are four dollars."

Sara told Cam, "I didn't take it."

"And I didn't either," Danny said.

"I know you didn't," Cam said.

She looked at the box. The only hole in it was the slit in the lid. On the table were some unsold tickets and two empty soda cans. Cam looked under the table. She found a ticket, but no money.

Danny told Cam, "Sara and I were both sitting here. We never left the room. Whenever we sold a ticket, we put the money in the box. And we never opened the box."

"I know," Cam said. "I just cut off the tape."

Cam opened the door to the auditorium. Cam, Sara, and Danny looked inside. At one side of the stage was an easel. A boy walked onto the stage and put a sign on the easel: HONEST ABE LINCOLN.

Cam whispered, "I must tell Ms. Benson about the missing money."

The curtain opened.

On the right of the stage was a very large cardboard box painted to look like the front of a house. In the center of the stage were two barrels and a table. There were lots of jars and small boxes on the table. Susie stood and looked at the things on the table. Above her was a sign: OFFUTT'S GENERAL STORE.

"I'll have to wait," Cam whispered. "I'll tell her after this scene."

Eric walked onto the stage. A spotlight followed him as he slowly walked toward Susie.

People in the audience applauded.

"Hello, Mrs. Olsen," Eric said.

Susie put her hand to her mouth.

"She's about to laugh," Sara whispered.

Susie looked to the right, to Ms. Benson offstage. Then she took her hand from her mouth and said, "Hello, Abe." She told Eric she needed flour, shortening, sugar, and raisins. She told him how much of each she needed. "I'm baking raisin bread," she said.

Eric carefully weighed each of the items. He wrapped them. He put everything in a large paper bag and gave it to Susie.

Eric took a small pad from his pocket. He made some notes on the pad and then told Susie, "That will be one dollar and nine cents."

Susie paid Eric. She walked to the right of the stage and sat by the cardboard house.

Other children came into Offutt's General Store.

"Abe, don't you have a story for us?" one of the children asked.

"Sure I do," Eric answered.

Eric told about a small child who was scared at night by a loud noise. "His father looked and looked," Eric said. "At last he

found the noise was coming from a bullfrog. He showed the boy the frog and said, 'Don't be scared, son. Sometimes a loud noise is just a way of saying *Howdy*.'"

Eric leaned back, opened his mouth, and laughed. The children on stage and lots of people in the audience laughed, too.

The children finished their shopping and left the store. Eric waited. When no one else came into the store, he counted the money he had been paid. He took the small pad from his pocket and looked at it.

"Oh my," he said. "Mrs. Olsen paid too much for her groceries."

"When he counted his money, he found too much," Danny whispered. "When we opened the shoe box and counted our money, we found too little."

Eric put lids on the barrels. He covered the table with a large cloth. Then he walked very slowly across the stage, toward Susie. He gave her a few coins.

Susie looked to the right again. Then she

said, "You walked all this way to bring me six cents?" She patted Eric's shoulder and said, "Now I know why people call you Honest Abe."

Eric and Susie walked to the center of the stage and bowed. The children who had been in Offutt's Store came out and bowed, too. People in the audience clapped.

As the curtain closed, Sara said to Cam and Danny, "This is a play about Honest

Abe Lincoln, but there's someone here who's not honest at all."

"He's not honest, but he's clever," Danny said. "Somehow, he stole the money without opening the box. And he stole the money without Sara or me seeing him do it."

"Ms. Benson said she was counting on me," Cam said, "and now the money is gone. I've got to tell her what happened."

CHAPTER FOUR

Cam hurried backstage. Ms. Benson was busy there, getting the stage and the children ready for the next scene.

"Clear the table. Move it to the side," Ms. Benson said. "Roll the barrels to the back of the stage. Take down the Offutt's sign and put up the LINCOLN FOR PRESIDENT sign."

"Ms. Benson," Cam said. "I have to talk to you."

"Good, Cam," Ms. Benson said. "I'm glad you're here. Make sure everyone is in place for the next scene."

"It's about the money," Cam said.

"Go ahead! Go ahead!" Ms. Benson told Cam. "Get everyone in place. The audience is waiting."

Everyone backstage was busy. Cam watched as the table and barrels were moved. Then someone brought out a small stepladder and placed it in the center of the stage.

Eric had on a top hat and a long black coat. He got up on the ladder. With one hand, he held onto the lapel of his coat. He pressed his lips together and tried to look very serious.

Cam stood to the right of Eric and called out, "Susie, Hillel, Jane, and Jacob. You belong here, facing Eric."

Then Cam went to Eric's left and called out, "Samuel and Deborah, you belong here."

"Are we set now?" Ms. Benson asked Cam. "Is everything OK?"

"The scene is ready," Cam told her. "But everything is *not* OK."

She told Ms. Benson there were only four dollars in the shoe box.

"What!" Ms. Benson said. "There should be lots more money than that."

Eric and the other children on stage heard Ms. Benson. They gathered around her, to hear what happened.

Cam told them all about the shoe box and the missing money.

"How could that happen?" Eric asked. "How could someone steal the money without opening the box?"

"What are we going to do?" Susie asked.

"Cam and I will find the money," Eric said. "This is a mystery and Cam and I will solve it. We solve lots of mysteries."

"You are not solving anything," Ms. Benson told Eric. "You're President Lincoln."

Ms. Benson looked at the children who had gathered around Cam. "Now, get to your places," Ms. Benson told them. "People came here to see a play, and they're going to

see one. We'll find the money."

Eric got back on the ladder. "Don't worry," he told everyone. "Cam will say, 'Click' a few times. She'll look at all those pictures she has in her head and find the money."

Ms. Benson took a small telephone from her pocket. She called the police and quickly told them what happened.

"Please, go outside and wait for the

police," Ms. Benson told Cam. "They will be here soon."

Then Ms. Benson called out, "Dim the lights!"

Cam hurried to the side of the stage. She watched the children in the center of the stage wait for the curtains to open. Then Cam looked to the back of the stage, at the Offutt's General Store sign, the table, and the barrels.

"Open the curtains!" Ms. Benson called out.

Cam looked at the table again. Suddenly, she remembered something. She closed her eyes and said, *"Click!"*

Cam said, *"Click!"* again.

She opened her eyes. "I just saw something," she told Ms. Benson. "I don't know who took the money, but I think I know when it was taken."

"That's a start," Ms Benson said. "Tell the police whatever you know."

"I will," Cam said, "but first, I have to talk to Sara and Danny."

CHAPTER FIVE

The curtains opened.

"A house divided against itself cannot stand," Eric called out. "This nation cannot survive half slave and half free."

Cam hurried down the aisle to the back of the auditorium. "I need to talk to you," she told Sara and Danny.

They followed Cam out of the auditorium.

"You said you never left the room, but you did. When I came back, there were two empty soda cans on the table."

Sara told Cam, "We didn't leave the room

to get the soda. A boy came in here with an ice cooler."

"There were only a few people in line," Danny added. "Some of them also bought soda."

"That's when the money was taken," Cam said. "The money was taken when there were four people still in line. They bought their tickets after the money was stolen. That's why, when I opened the box, there were only four dollars in it."

Cam looked outside. There were still many children in the playground. She saw a boy with a large cooler sitting under a tree in the corner of the school yard.

Cam pointed to the boy sitting under the tree. "Did he sell you the soda?" Cam asked.

Sara and Danny looked at the boy.

"That's him," they told Cam.

Just then there were flashing lights. A police car parked near the school yard. Two officers got out, a man and a woman.

Cam ran to them.

"I'm Officer Feldman," the woman said, "and this is my partner, Officer Zuto."

Cam pointed to the boy sitting under the tree. "That boy may be the thief," she told the officers. "He may be the one who stole the ticket money."

"We have to speak with Ms. Benson," Officer Zuto told Cam. "Is she inside?"

"I'll take you to her," Sara said.

The two officers started to follow Sara and Danny.

"Wait!" Cam said. "Can't one of you stay with me and watch the thief?"

"I'll stay," Officer Feldman said.

Cam told her about the play, the almost empty shoe box, and the boy with the ice cooler.

"Let's talk to him," Officer Feldman said. "Let's see what he knows about the missing money."

Cam and Officer Feldman walked across the playground.

"Do you want a soda?" the boy asked.

"No," Officer Feldman answered. "We want to talk to you."

The school doors opened. Officer Zuto came out. He was followed by Sara, Danny, and Ms. Benson.

"That's him," Sara told Ms. Benson. She pointed to the boy sitting under the tree. "He's the one!"

CHAPTER SIX

"What's going on?" the boy asked. "What did I do?"

"Did you go into the school?" Officer Feldman asked.

"I went in there to sell soda," the boy answered. "That's what I always do."

"And what about the money?" Officer Zuto asked. "Did you go near the table? Did you go near the shoe box?"

"Excuse me. Please, excuse me," a girl said. "I'm thirsty. I'd like an orange soda."

Everyone waited and watched while the boy reached into the cooler. It was filled with ice and lots of cans. The boy found an orange soda. He gave it to the girl and she paid him.

"Do you always do that?" Ms. Benson asked. "Do you always find the sodas?"

"No one else knows my system," the boy answered. "Watch this," the boy said. "I'll get a cola."

He closed his eyes. Then he lifted the top off the cooler and reached in. He took out a can and said, "Cola."

He was right.

He put that back. With his eyes still closed, he took out another can and said, "Ginger ale."

He was right again.

He opened his eyes. "I know where everything is," he said proudly. "I can reach in and find any kind of soda you want."

"When you came into the school," Ms. Benson asked, "did you stay by the cooler?"

"Yes," the boy answered. "I always do."

"But when you got your drinks," Ms. Benson said to Sara and Danny, "you weren't by the table. That's when someone stole from the shoe box."

"The shoe box," Cam said. She thought for a moment. "The shoe box," she said again. Then Cam closed her eyes and said, *"Click!"*

"What happened when you came into the school?" Officer Feldman asked.

"People crowded around me. They all bought drinks," the boy answered.

"Did you see anyone else come into the school? Did you see anyone go to the table?"

Cam said, *"Click!"* again.

"No," the boy answered. "But I wasn't watching the table."

"Click!"

"What's all this clicking?" Ms. Benson asked Cam. "Do you remember something?"

"Yes," Cam answered and opened her eyes. "You keep asking about your shoe box. But that's not the one I opened."

"Sure it is," Danny said. "I saw you do it. I saw you cut the tape and take out four dollars."

"I saw it, too," Sara said.

Ms. Benson lifted her right foot and said, "These shoes came in that box. They're new."

"No," Cam insisted. "I *didn't* cut tape off your shoe box. Wait right here and I'll prove it."

CHAPTER SEVEN

Cam hurried across the playground. She went into the school and found the box and the lid. They were still on the table. Cam looked at them carefully, to see if they matched the picture she had in her head.

They did.

Cam grabbed the box and the lid. She ran outside and gave them to Officer Feldman.

"That isn't the shoe box Ms. Benson left on the table," Cam said. "It's a sneaker box, a size ten sneaker box."

"And I didn't wrap the whole box in tape

like that," Ms. Benson said. "I taped it neatly, along the sides."

"Whoever stole the money," Cam said, "switched the boxes."

"Did you see anyone come into the school with this box?" Officer Feldman asked Sara and Danny.

They both said they hadn't.

"So," Ms. Benson said, "we know when and how the money was stolen. What we need to know is who did it. If we knew that, maybe we'd get the money back."

Officer Feldman took the sneaker box and said, "That's true, but we do know a few things about the thief."

"The thief," Cam said quickly, "is a boy with a new pair of blue, size ten sneakers."

Ms. Benson looked at the box. "And these are expensive sneakers," she said. "I bet he's very proud of them. I bet that right now, he's wearing them."

"Let's start looking," Officer Zuto said.

"Wait," Cam said to the two police officers. "If the thief sees you here, he might get scared and run off. Then we may never find him. I'll look for him."

"And I'll help," Ms. Benson said. "He never saw me. He won't know I'm from the school."

"We'll give you a few minutes," Officer Feldman told Cam and Ms. Benson. "We'll wait here, under the tree. Then, if you don't find him, we'll look, too."

Sara and Danny waited with the two police officers. Cam and Ms. Benson walked slowly through the playground and looked for a boy wearing a new pair of size ten blue sneakers.

Ms. Benson pointed to a boy on the swings. "He's wearing blue sneakers," she said.

"He can't be the thief," Cam said. "He's too young. Those sneakers are probably size two."

There were many children, mostly boys, playing basketball.

"You know, he may not be here," Ms. Benson told Cam.

Cam stopped and said, "Wait a minute. I may know what he looks like."

Cam closed her eyes. She said, *"Click!"*

"Some boys came into the school," Cam said, with her eyes closed. "They wanted to know what we were doing. I told them about the play, but they weren't interested. One said he learned enough about President Lincoln in school."

"Oh, no," Ms. Benson said. "You can never learn enough about President Lincoln."

"One of those boys must have seen Sara and Danny put money into the shoe box. He must live near here. He went home. He taped up the sneaker box. Then, when he saw the boy go in with the cooler, he sneaked in and switched the boxes."

"Was one of them wearing blue sneakers?" Ms. Benson asked.

"Yes," Cam said with her eyes still closed.

"A tall boy with long blond hair had blue sneakers on. And he wore a white T-shirt and black pants."

Cam opened her eyes. She looked among the many boys playing basketball. "There he is," Cam said, and pointed. "There's the thief. Let's go get him."

CHAPTER EIGHT

"Are you sure he's the thief?" Ms. Benson asked.

"Yes, I'm sure. Now let's go get him."

"No," Ms. Benson said. "That's a job for the police."

Cam and Ms. Benson went to the corner of the school yard, where the police officers were waiting. Cam pointed to the boy. She explained why she was sure he was the thief.

Officer Feldman walked directly toward the boy. Cam, Ms. Benson, Sara, and Danny followed her. Officer Zuto went the other way. He wanted to be on the other side of the playground, in case the boy turned and ran.

The boy with blue sneakers was running toward the basket. Another boy had the ball. He threw the ball to the basket and missed. The boy with blue sneakers jumped. He got the ball. He turned to pass the ball and saw Officer Feldman. The boy quickly turned and ran the other way, right into the arms of Officer Zuto.

"We need to talk to you," Officer Zuto said.

"About what? I'm playing basketball. Is there some law against that?"

"There is a law against stealing," Ms.

Benson said. "And you stole money we raised for charity."

"You have no proof I stole anything," the boy said.

"Those sneakers you're wearing are proof," Officer Feldman told him. She showed him the box and said, "This is the box they came in."

The boy looked at the box. Then he looked at his sneakers.

"OK! OK! I'll give the money back," the boy said. "I'm sorry. I'll give it all back."

There were two large zippered pockets on the front of the boy's pants. He reached down and opened them. He took out lots of bills and coins. He gave them all to Officer Feldman. She gave them to Ms. Benson.

"Can I go now?" the boy asked.

"No, I'm sorry," Officer Zuto said. "You did something terribly wrong. We're taking you to the police station."

"Wait," Ms. Benson said. "First, I want him to see something."

CHAPTER NINE

Everyone followed Ms. Benson to the front of the auditorium. A sign, THE GETTYSBURG ADDRESS, was on the easel. Now Eric wore a stick-on beard. He stood on the small stepladder.

"That this nation," Eric was saying, "under God, shall have a new birth of freedom, and that government of the people, by the people, for the people, shall not perish from the earth."

People in the audience stood and cheered. Eric got off the ladder and bowed to the audience. The other children on stage bowed, too. The play was done.

"Wait!" Ms. Benson called out. "There's more."

"There is?" Sara asked.

Ms. Benson hurried onto the stage. She spoke to the children. The curtain closed. People in the audience sat and waited.

"What is she doing?" Officer Zuto asked.

"I don't know," Cam answered. "Ms. Benson likes to surprise us."

Everyone waited. Then the curtain opened.

The stage was set again for the first scene, "Honest Abe Lincoln."

Eric walked slowly toward Susie. "Hello, Mrs. Olsen," Eric said to her.

Susie put her hand to her mouth. She looked to the right of the stage. Cam heard Ms. Benson whisper, "No laughing onstage. Don't laugh!"

Susie took her hand from her mouth and said, "Hello, Abe."

When the scene was done, people in the audience stood again and cheered.

Ms. Benson thanked the police officers. Then she told the boy who had stolen the money, "I hope you watched that. You can learn a lesson from Honest Abe Lincoln."

Officers Feldman and Zuto took the boy who had stolen the money into their police car. They drove off.

Cam went backstage. Her parents were there with Eric and his family.

Eric told Cam, "I knew you would *click* and find the thief."

Cam said, "And I knew you would be a great President Lincoln."

Eric smiled.

"You really were great," Cam's parents, Eric's parents, and Donna and Diane said.

"Maybe I was good," Eric said, "but I'm happy to be Eric Shelton again." He reached into his pocket and took out his stick-on beard. "This itches."

Then, with the beard, Eric teased his sisters. He tickled Donna and Diane's noses.

"Hey," Donna said, "that does itch."

Diane giggled and said, "And it tickles."

Donna and Diane laughed.

Diane took the stick-on beard and put it on. "I'm President Lincoln's sister," she said. "Don't I look like him?"

"That's funny," Eric said and laughed. "That's very funny," he said. Then Eric leaned back, opened his mouth wide, and laughed. It was his great President Lincoln laugh.

When Cam, her parents, the Sheltons,

and Ms. Benson heard Eric laugh, they laughed, too. Soon everyone in the auditorium was laughing. They all laughed along with Eric Shelton, the star of the play *Stories of President Lincoln*.

The End

A Cam Jansen Memory Game

Take another look at the picture on page 5. Study it. Blink your eyes and say, *"Click!"* Then turn back to this page and answer these questions—remember, don't peek at the questions before you study the picture.

1. How many people are in the picture?
2. Who's wearing polka dots?
3. What is Sara reading?
4. Who is wearing glasses?
5. What book is Danny holding?
6. How many books are on the table?